T0147077

INTO HIS PRESENCE
"INSTRUCTOR'S STUDY GUIDE"

Tabernacle & The Priesthood

BOBBY HOLMES

WESTBOW
PRESS*
A DIVISION OF THOMAS NELSON
& ZONDERVAN

WestBow Press books may be ordered through booksellers or by contacting:

WestBow Press
A Division of Thomas Nelson & Zondervan
1663 Liberty Drive
Bloomington, IN 47403
www.westbowpress.com
844-714-3454

All Scripture quotations are taken from the King James Version.

ISBN: 978-1-6642-6687-2 (sc)
ISBN: 978-1-6642-6688-9 (hc)
ISBN: 978-1-6642-6689-6 (e)

Print information available on the last page.

WestBow Press rev. date: 05/13/2022

The Lord Bless Thee and Keep Thee:
The Lord Make His Face Shine Upon Thee:
The Lord Lift Up His Countenance Upon Thee,
And Give Thee Peace.

Numbers 6:24-26

Jesus spoke these words over His disciples just before He was parted from them and carried up into Heaven. (Luke 24:50 & 51)

Fulfilling the duties of the High Priest and of His Father's Word. (Numbers 6:24-26)

I pray God's blessings upon you as you study God's Word and dig deep beneath the surface of God's Word that you might draw close to Him. Don't let anything stop you from coming to know Him and the power of His resurrection.

Live in His resurrection power, walk in the newness of life that God has given you. Sit together with God in Heavenly places, you've been washed in the blood of Jesus and have been made worthy to be in His presence for the purpose of praise, worship and intercession for others.

Bless the Lord with the fruit of your lips giving thanks unto God and the lifting up of your hands as the evening sacrifices. Praise Him from the depths of your heart, from your inner being, and walk with Him in His glory.

You've not only been freed from sin and its power broken off of you but, even your conscience has been purged from dead works that you can serve the Living God.

This means you've been made free you've been forgiven; let it go, walk away from it, leave it behind you. You don't have to carry the burden of those sins any longer. Jesus bore them and lifted them off of us. Accept His blessings of deliverance and worship Him freely. Enter into the presence of God. He has given you this liberty, live in oneness with God; in agreement with Him.

Proverbs 4:7 – Wisdom is the principal thing; therefore, get wisdom: and with all thy getting get understanding.

CONTENTS

CHAPTER 1

The Law of God and
The Tabernacle

God told Moses to come up to Mount Sinai to receive the Commandments, the tablets of stone that he could teach to the children of Israel (Exodus 24:12).

As God began to speak to Moses in chapter 25, and for the next six chapters, God showed Moses the tabernacle and described each part of it with great detail. Nothing is mentioned about God's laws until Exodus 31:18. This is when God gave Moses the two tablets of stone written with the finger of God when he was done communing with him.

The majority of the time was spent showing Moses the tabernacle because Moses had to build the tabernacle just like the one he was being shown, for it was going to be a dwelling place for the Spirit of

God, as well as a way to bring forth sacrifice, offering, praise, and worship.

God's law was of no less importance, for how can one come into the presence of God without obedience to His Word?

First Samuel 15:22 states, "And Samuel said, 'Hath the Lord as great delight in burnt offerings and sacrifices, as in obeying the voice of the Lord? Behold to obey is better than sacrifice, and to hearken than the fat of rams.'"

John 14:21 says, "He that hath my commandments, and keep them, he it is that loveth me: and he loveth me shall be loved of my Father, and I will love him, and will manifest myself to him."

John 14:23 says, "Jesus answered and said unto him, 'If a man love me, he will keep my words: and my Father will love him, and we will come unto him, and make our abode with him.'"

Obeying God's Word is a fully expected requirement. Obedience to God's Word takes place first before you can present your body as a living sacrifice, holy and acceptable to God, which is your reasonable service (Romans 12:1).

Obey God, love God, and praise and worship our God! Keep on keeping on for Jesus!

📖 Questions

1) What were the two reasons God told Moses to come up to Mount Sinai?

   Answer 1: To receive the laws of God so that he may teach them to the people (Exodus 24:12).

   Answer 2: To receive instructions to build the tabernacle, a dwelling place for the very presence of God (Exodus 25:8–9).

   "God was establishing Obedience, Sacrifice, Offerings, Praise and Worship; a way for man to have fellowship with God and to come into His presence."

2) What was Moses instructed to do when he came up to Mount Sinai?

   Answer: Be there (Exodus 24:12).

   "To be there in the Glory of God."

3) In your opinion, what was the purpose of being six days early?

   Answer: First, to prepare to be with God; second, to be set apart; and third, to empty out oneself.

4) Moses obeyed God and went up to Mount Sinai. What took place in order for Moses to meet God?

Answer: Moses went into the midst of the Cloud of Glory and God gat him up to the mount.

Gat (5927)—a departure in a northerly direction; an ascension to a higher place.

5) Moses was in Mount Sinai for forty days and forty nights. How long was he with God, being shown the tabernacle and all its furnishings?

Answer: Thirty-three days (Exodus 24:16–18).

6) What specific way was Moses instructed to build the tabernacle?

Answer: "According to all that I show thee, after the pattern of the Tabernacle and the pattern of all the instruments thereof, even so shall ye make it" (Exodus 25:9).

7) Why was it so important to build the tabernacle exactly like the one God showed to Moses in the mount?

Answer 1: The tabernacle had to be built exactly like the true tabernacle that the Lord pitched, not humans (Hebrews 8:2).

Answer 2: So that the glory of God would fill the tabernacle (Exodus 25:8–9, 40:33–35).

Dick Reuben, a Jewish Christian preacher said, "When the pattern is right, the glory will fall."

CHAPTER 2

Who Built the Tabernacle?

Moses received the instructions to build the tabernacle and was the overseer of it. It was to be built according to the pattern shown to him in the mount. God chose two men and told Moses their names while in Mount Sinai.

1) What were their names, and what did their names mean?

    Answer 1: Bezaleel (1212), meaning "in the shadow of God."

    Answer 2: Aholiab (171), meaning "tent of his Father."

    (Exodus 31:2, 6)

"We must be in the Shadow of God, to be our Father's tent (Tabernacle)."

God said, "Let them make me a Sanctuary: that I may dwell among them" (Exodus 25:8).

God chose Bezaleel and Aholiab but also in the hearts of all that are wise hearted I have put wisdom, that they make all that I have commanded them (Exodus 31:6, 35:34–35).

First Corinthians 6:19 says, "What? Know ye not that your body is the temple of the Holy Ghost which is in you, which ye have of God, and ye are not your own?"

CHAPTER 3

How Was the Tabernacle Built?

It was the Spirit of God that enabled Bezaleel, Aholiab, and all those who were wise-hearted to build such a place of great detail for the very presence of God to dwell in.

1) What four things did they receive of the Spirit of God?

   Answer 1: Wisdom.

   Answer 2: Understanding.

   Answer 3: Knowledge.

   Answer 4: Workmanship.

2) Who built the true tabernacle? Give the chapter and verse.

Answer: The Lord (Hebrews 8:2).

3) How does building the tabernacle relate to us?

Answer 1: The materials were a free will offering from a willing-hearted people.

Answer 2: It had to be built according to the patterns of God's Word.

Answer 3: It was the Spirit of God that enabled them to build such a place of great detail.

Answer 4: It was a dwelling place for the Holy Spirit of God.

CHAPTER 4

The Courtyard Fence

The courtyard fence surrounded the tabernacle, brazen altar, and the laver. It was a barrier to the children of Israel encamped round about. It was seven feet, six inches tall, which means they couldn't see over it, and they were to pitch their tents far off about the tabernacle. It was to set apart the courtyard as holy ground from the rest of the camp.

God is holy and desires to be among His people, so He designed a place in which they could be made holy and have fellowship with Him.

The courtyard fence was 100 cubits by 50 cubits by 5 cubits tall, the circumference being 300 cubits times 5 cubits tall, equaling 1,500 cubits. God gave Moses the law in approximately 1500 BC. The courtyard fence represents the law. Let's do a breakdown of each part of the fence and see not only the law of God but also the love and grace of God.

1) What did the wood post represent?

   Answer: Humanity (Mark 8:24 and Isaiah 61:3).

2) What was the post overlaid with, and what did it represent?

   Answer: Brass or copper, which represent judgment. The sockets or bases of the post were also made of solid brass or copper. The courtyard fence was covered with a white fine-twined linen curtain.

3) What was the curtain attached to?

   Answer: Silver hooks and fillets of silver (Exodus 27:10).

4) What's the Hebrew definition of *fillets* in Exodus 27:10 (2838)?

   Answer: A fillet (2838) is a fence, rail, or rod connecting the post or pillars.

The courtyard fence was built this same way on each side, and the entry gate was attached this same way.

Exodus 27:17–19 gives a summary of how the fence was made.

5) What does the phrase *filleted* (2836) *with silver* mean in the original Hebrew language from verse 17?

Answer: *Filleted* (2836) means to be attached to, to love, or to have pleasure in. It has the sense of joining together, adhering, or cleaving. This kind of love is already bound to its object.

This is where we should be able to see that we're really not just reading about a courtyard fence. God is describing His love for His people, a type of love that loves us before we even know Him.

Romans 5:8 says, "But God commandeth His love toward us, in that, while we were yet sinners, Christ died for us."

The filleted silver rod went through every hook or ring that was attached to each part of the fence, attaching one to another and creating a strong enclosure for the courtyard. Each and every post was important, for it helped to support the others next to it.

6) Each post had something on top of it. What was it, and what did it represent?

Answer: Wooden chapiters overlaid with silver, which represented the humanity of Christ and the redemption of our salvation (Exodus 38:17).

Ephesians 4:15–16 says, "But speaking the Truth in love, may grow up into Him in all things, which is the head, even Christ."

From whom the whole body fitly joined together and compacted by that which every joint supplieth, according to the effectual working in the measure of every part, maketh increase of the body unto the edifying of itself in love.

7) With our study of each part of the courtyard fence, write a summary of God's revelation that you can see in the scriptures as you look on the courtyard fence and explain what He's clothed you in.

(Refer to the first paragraph of the chapter on the courtyard fence.)

Answer: The courtyard fence is a beautiful picture of God's love for the Old Testament church and of us in the new covenant church being unable to fulfill the whole law of God. We are bound by our own sin and stand under the judgment of God. Yet we are delivered by Jesus, the head of the church, as He commits Himself to us with a love that covers all sin and shortcomings, as well as clothes us in His righteousness.

CHAPTER 5

The Entrance of the Courtyard

There's not much written about the gate of the courtyard fence in the book *Into His Presence*, but that's not because it's not important. The gate was made of the same material as the door; first hanging and the veil of the tabernacle, which we know represents Jesus's body. We study these colors of linen as we study the veil.

1) What was the size of each side of the gate and the fence?

   Answer 1: The gate was twenty cubits (thirty feet).

   Answer 2: The fence was fifteen cubits (twenty-two feet, six inches) on each side.

   Answer 3: Both the gate and the fence were five cubits tall.

Exodus 27:14–16

The Courtyard Fence was to create a barrier from the encampment of the children of Israel, for the Courtyard to be set apart as Holy Ground.

2) *The Gate being the only way into the Courtyard would remind us of what scripture?*

Answer: John 14:6 - Jesus said, "I am the Way, the Truth and the Life, no man cometh unto the Father but by me".

Jesus fulfilled the Law and therefore the Gate representing Jesus' body was able to become a part of this Fence and provide a way into the Courts of the Lord.

CHAPTER 6

The Brazen Altar

As you come through the Gate of the Courtyard Fence, the first thing you'll see is the Brazen Altar, which represents Jesus and is a place of sacrifice.

Even so as we come to Jesus for Salvation, we come to the place of the Cross, a place of sacrifice.

John 10: 17,18 – "Therefore doth my Father love me, because I lay down my life, that I might take it again. No man taketh it from me, but I lay it down of myself. I have power to lay it down, and I have power to take it again. This commandment have I received of my Father."

We also must be willing to lay our life down spiritually and take on the newness of life, through the power of His resurrection by the blood of Jesus.

1) *The Brazen Altar was made of* _____
   _____ *and overlayed with* _____, *which
   represents* _____.

   Exodus 27:1,2

   Answer 1: ShittimWood

   Answer 2: Brass or Copper

   Answer 3: Judgment

2) *What was the size of the Brazen Altar?*

   *Answer: 5 cubits (7 feet, 6 inches) wide by 3 cubits (4 feet, 6
   inches) tall*

   (Exodus 27:1)

3) *What's the size of the Brazen Altar and the way it was built
   symbolic of?*

   Answer 1: Hebrews 2 14-18 – Jesus took on humanity.

   Answer 2: John 10:17,18 – Jesus laid down his life.

   *Answer 3: II Corinthians 5:21 - For He hath made Him to
   be sin for us, who knew no sin; that we might be made the
   righteousness of God in Him.*

4) *There was a Grate of Network of Brass for the Brazen Altar. Where was the Grate placed?*

Answer: under the Compass of the Altar beneath (on each side of the altar) Exodus 27:5

5) *What was the Grate of Network of Brass for?*

Answer 1: Grate (4345) a covering

Answer 2: Network (4640) operative, exerting power or force

Answer 3: The Grate was a protective covering for the Altar because the animals of sacrifice would kick against it.

6) *What did it represent?*

Answer: Judgment

Jesus bore the judgment of God upon every side, from the North, South, East and West; for all people.

Hebrews 9:27-28 - and as it is appointed unto men once to die, but after this the judgment: so Christ was once offered to bear the sins of many; and unto them that look for Him shall He appear the second time without sin unto Salvation.

You see why it's so important to place the Grate of Network of brass round about the outside of the altar, beneath the Compass as scripture says; instead of going with logic and placing it inside the altar for a place for the animal sacrifices to be laid on. There's been many pictures that show this but that's not what scripture says and it's for a reason. God is a God of details and he's done it all for us.

There's much more to share about the Brazen Altar, let's continue to see God's love for us as we study.

7) *What is the Compass of the Altar?*

Answer: Compass (3749) a rim, top margin (ledge)

The Compass of the Altar was a ledge that went round about the altar on every side and the Grate of Network of brass was placed just beneath it at the midst of the altar.

In order for us to see the purpose of the Compass of the Altar, the ledge, we need to study the sacrifices in Leviticus Chapter 1:4-9. There's a lot of detail to go over in these verses. Let's take the time to study and see God's love for us in these scriptures.

8) *When someone brought an offering unto the Lord, who took the life of the animal sacrifice?*

   Answer: The person that brought the sacrifice placed his hand upon the head of the offering and he would also take its life. (Leviticus 1:4-5)

   The priest would take the blood from the sacrifice and sprinkle (2236) it round about the Brazen Altar. (Sprinkle 2236 – to pour out)

9) *The blood was poured out round about the altar against the Grate of Network of brass and no doubt against the altar itself. What was this symbolic of?*

   Answer: It creates an unbreakable bond between God and man because there's no greater sacrifice.

   This is found when you look up the word Sprinkle (2236) in the Hebrew language.

   The Grate of Network of brass which represents judgment was covered with the blood of the sacrifice. (Hebrews 9:27-28)

10) *Knowing the Brazen Altar was hollow on the inside according to Exodus 27:8 and the Grate of Network of Brass was on the*

outside of the altar, how was the sacrifice placed upon the altar?

Answer: The sacrifice was cut in pieces for the purpose of cleansing and placed in order upon the altar, as the wood was placed in order to hold the sacrifice. (Leviticus 1:6-9)

We see again the importance of the Grate of Network of Brass being on the outside of the Brazen Altar, beneath the Compass round about. Everything within the Tabernacle of the Old Testament was a shadow of that which was to come.

God showed me the order of the wood was in order to hold the sacrifice, which was symbolic of that which was to come. When Jesus was placed upon the cross the wood was placed in order to hold the sacrifice!

Remembering the Brazen Altar was 7 feet 6 inches square and 4 feet 6 inches tall, which is a good size altar.

11) *How was the sacrifice placed in order upon the wood and how did they reach that far?*

Answer: They would have to get upon the ledge of the altar and walk around it on each side to be able to do this. (Leviticus 9:22)

12) *Once the High Priest was finished offering the sacrifices upon the Brazen Altar, what would he do before coming down?*

Answer: Aaron lifted his hand toward the people and blessed them with the Priestly Blessing. (Leviticus 9:22, see Numbers 6:24-27)

13) *What was this symbolic of?*

Answer: Jesus led them out as far as to Bethany, and He lifted up His hands and blessed them.

And it came to pass, while He blessed them, He was parted from them, and carried up into Heaven. (Luke 24:50-51)

CHAPTER 7

The Priesthood

The Priesthood wasn't passed down to you and placed entirely upon your shoulders; you were brought into a Royal Priesthood, where Jesus is our Great High Priest of an everlasting Priesthood after the order of Melchizedek.

You are blessed, you've been chosen and permitted to come into God's presence not only for ourselves but also for others.

1) *Where is the scripture that says the Priesthood will be established with Aaron and his sons as an everlasting Priesthood and why?*

Answer 1: Numbers 25:13

Answer 2: Phinehas was zealous for God.

2) *What was the purpose of the Priesthood?*

Answer: Aaron, his sons and his father's house with him were to bear (5375) the iniquity of the Sanctuary and of the Priesthood. (Numbers 18:1)

Bear (5375) to lift, carry or pardon

3) *Write a summary of what it means to bear the iniquity of the Sanctuary and the Priesthood.*

Answer: To bear the sin of the people, to carry the weight of their guilt and shame. To make sacrifice and present the shed blood before God for an atonement, which was a shadow of the shed blood of Christ, which was to come.

To be involved in someone's life, to show compassion, mercy and understanding with the purpose of restoration.

4) *God gave the Priesthood to them as a service gift. What service was expected of them?*

Answer: They were to keep charge of the Sanctuary, everything of the Altar and within the Veil. (Numbers 18:5-7)

5) *Tracking the Priesthood down through the generations shown in I Chronicles, chapter 24; the descendants of Aaron. Who*

is a direct descendent of Aaron according to scripture in the New Testament?

Answer: Zacharias was a priest of the course of Abia ; a descendent of Aaron shown in I Chronicles 24:10. Elizabeth, his wife, was of the daughters of Aaron. (Luke 1:5)

This placed John the Baptist as a direct descendent of Aaron to be brought into the Levitical Priesthood.

Jesus said John was more than a prophet. "For this is he, of whom it is written, behold, I send my messenger before thy face, which shall prepare thy way before thee." (Matthew 11:9-10)

The angel, Gabriel, that stands in the presence of God, told Zacharias that John would be great in the sight of God and would be filled with the Holy Ghost even from his mother's womb. John would turn many of the children of Israel to the Lord, showing them the way, and to make ready a people prepared for the Lord.

Jesus and the angel, Gabriel, said that John would prepare the way and turn many of the children of Israel to the Lord; to make ready a people prepared for the Lord.

6) *What Old Testament scripture does this seem to fulfill having to do with the Priesthood?*

Answer: Numbers 18:1

The Holy Ghost of God has moved upon me to write about the change that's taking place from the Old Testament Priesthood to the New Testament Priesthood. This is not written in the book, Into His Presence, this was just impressed upon my heart.

The Priesthood of the Old Testament accepted sacrifices and offerings of the children of Israel. Life was taken and the blood was offered up before God for an atonement and poured out round about the Brazen Altar; creating the symbolic, unbreakable bond between God and man.

John the Baptist, being filled with the Holy Ghost, even from his mother's womb; was ordained to prepare the way of the Lord, make his paths straight.

The Word of God came unto him while in the wilderness and John came into all the country about Jordan, preaching the baptism of repentance for the remission of sins.

The voice of him that crieth in the wilderness, "prepare ye the way of the Lord, make straight in the desert a highway for our God. Every valley shall be exalted and every mountain and hill shall be made low: and the crooked shall be made straight, and the rough places plain: and the Glory of the Lord shall be revealed, and all flesh shall see it together; for the mouth of the Lord hath spoken it. (Isaiah 40:3-5)

The fullness of time, of God's calling upon John's life was come; being filled with the Holy Ghost he began to proclaim the goodness and Glory of God. Preaching repentance for the remission of sins.

No offerings or sacrifices were being brought to him, yet the people asked John, "What shall we do?"

God's Word was being preached through the power of the Holy Ghost and the people were being drawn closer to God; as John preached and proclaimed: "Behold the Lamb of God, which taketh away the sin of the world". John showed them the salvation that had come.

Jesus came as the Lamb of God to take away the sin of the world. He also took on the Priesthood of an endless life to save us to the uttermost, forever more making a way for us to enter into the holiest by the blood of Jesus, by a new and living way which He has consecrated for us, through the veil, that is to say His flesh.

By the which we are sanctified through the offering of the body of Jesus Christ once for all. (Hebrews 10:10)

7) *Why did John the Baptist, baptize Jesus?*

Answer: To fulfill (4137) all righteousness (1343).

Fulfill (4137) spoken of duty or obligation

Righteousness (1343) of actions, duties, what is right, proper, fit

(Matthew 3:15)

John said, "He must increase but I must decrease".

The Priesthood was passed down to Jesus through the baptism of John, even as Moses washed Aaron and his sons at the door of the Tabernacle and clothed them in the Priestly Garments.

8) What Priestly Garment was Jesus clothed with?

Answer: The Holy Ghost (John 1:32)

The Robe of the Ephod, "spiritually".

Think of it, the Everlasting Priesthood that God had established with man through the tribe of Levi has made a change to the tribe of Judah, in which Jesus was born and has now taken the position of our Great High Priest after the order of Melchizedek, the power of an endless life: He ever lives to make intercession for us before God the Father.

Jesus has taken the reins, He's at the front leading the way. He's the minister of the Sanctuary and of the True Tabernacle which the Lord pitched, not man. (Hebrews 8:2)

Jesus presented Himself before God the Father as the offering of First Fruits after His resurrection. Presenting Himself alive, clean, pure and unspotted of any defilement; that as he was accepted before the Father as the First Fruits, even so we who are still to come will be accepted in the beloved.

Wherefore, in all things it behooved Him to be made like unto his brethren, that he might be a merciful and faithful High Priest in things pertaining to God, to make reconciliation for the sins of the people.

For in that He himself hath suffered being tempted, He is able to succour them that are tempted. (Hebrews 2:17-18)

For Christ is not entered into the holy places made with hands, which are the figures of the true; but into heaven itself, now to appear in the presence of God for us. (Hebrews 9:24)

We are still to approach God as it's been written, but today we are to bring spiritual sacrifices and offerings; a broken heart and a contrite spirit if there's something that troubles you. The lifting up of our hands and the fruit of our lips giving thanks unto Him.

CHAPTER 8

The Church being Consecrated
into the Priesthood

Jesus knowing he had all authority, all power and the blessed assurance of His Father's voice after His baptism by John which said, "This is my beloved son, in whom I am well pleased". (Matthew 3:17)

Jesus knew that His hour had come, to return to His Father, and proceeded to fulfill His Father's Word.

1) What did Jesus do with the disciples after supper?

Answer: He riseth from supper, and laid aside (5087) His garments; and took a towel and girded Himself. After that He poureth water into a bason, and began to wash the disciple's feet, and to wipe them with the towel wherewith He was girded. (John 13:4-5)

Laid aside (5087) to place in the sense of to lay off or aside, such as garments.

This term also refers to setting one in place or ordain. To place one into a position of privilege or ministry: although there is no scripture reference listed in the Greek concordance for this particular scripture. My thoughts are this is the dedication into the Priesthood.

2) What's the overall concept of what is being done here?

Answer: "If I then, your Lord and Master, have washed your feet; ye also ought to wash one another's feet." (See John 13:13-17)

The reference scriptures to verse 14: "ye also ought to wash one another's feet". (Romans 12:10, Galatians 6:1-2, I Peter 5:5)

Romans 12:10 – Be kindly affectioned one to another with brotherly love; in honor preferring one another.

Galatians 6:1-2 – Brethren, if a man be overtaken in a fault, ye which are spiritual, restore such a one in the spirit of meekness; considering thyself, lest thou also be tempted. Bear ye one another's burdens, and so fulfill the law of Christ.

I Peter 5:5 – Likewise, ye younger, submit yourselves unto the elder. Yea, all of you be subject one to another, and be clothed with humility; for God resisteth the proud, and giveth grace to the humble.

3) What Old Testament scripture having to do with the Priesthood do these scriptures remind you of?

Answer: And the Lord said unto Aaron, thou and thy sons and thy father's house with thee shall bear the iniquity of the Sanctuary: and thou and thy sons with thee shall bear the iniquity of your Priesthood.

4) What type of service does God consider the Priesthood to be?

Answer: I have given your Priest's office unto you as a Service Gift. (Numbers 18:7)

Read Numbers 18:1-7

The Priest were the only ones allowed inside the Tabernacle and also to tend to the altar with the sacrifices and all of the furniture inside the Holy Place as well as the Holy of Holies. The stranger that cometh nigh would be put to death.

Brothers and sisters, you've been brought into this Priesthood for a purpose. You are to bear ye one another's burdens and yet all the more for those who do not yet know our Lord and Savior, the Lord Jesus Christ.

You are to bring them before God, bear their load; consider where they are at and where you've been: bring them to Jesus!

You've been given access, into His presence and if they've not been washed in the blood of Jesus, then they have not received this access.

We will continue this subject as we move forward to the other chapters.

5) What about those of us beyond the day of the Cross? How are we brought into the Priesthood?

Answer 1: Through a blood birth.

Answer 2: Washed by the water of the Word.

Ephesians 5:26-27

John 19:34 – but one of the soldiers with a spear pierced His side, and forthwith came there out blood and water.

Hebrews 10:22 – Let us draw near with a true heart in full assurance of faith, having our hearts sprinkled from an evil conscience and our bodies washed with pure water.

CHAPTER 9

The Garments of the Priesthood

1) Who was to be clothed in the Garments of the Priesthood?

   Answer: Aaron and his sons (Exodus 28:4)

2) What did God say the Garments were for? (2 purposes)

   Answer 1: for Glory (3519) and for beauty (Exodus 28:2)

   Answer 2: To consecrate him, that he may minister unto me in the Priest's office. (Exodus 28:3)

3) Name the Garments.

   Answer 1: Linen Breeches (Exodus 28:42)

Answer 2: Breastplate, "Breastplate of Judgment"

Ephod

Robe, "Robe of the Ephod"

Broidered Coat "White Robe of Righteousness)

Mitre

Girdle

(Exodus 28:4)

4) How was Aaron and his sons hallowed, consecrated into the Priesthood?

Answer 1: Sacrifice

Answer 2: Moses washed them at the door of the Tabernacle.

Answer 3: Moses put the Garments upon them.

5) Did Moses put all the Garments upon them?

Answer: No, they put the Linen Breeches on themselves. (Exodus 28:43)

6) What does the Linen Breeches and the white linen Broidered Coat represent?

Answer: He hath clothed me with the Garment of Salvation, he hath covered me with the Robe of Righteousness. (Isaiah 61:10)

They ministered unto the Lord by keeping charge of the Sanctuary, everything of the Brazen Altar, and within the Veil.

CHAPTER 10

Garments of the High Priest

1) What Priestly Garments and other items did the High Priest wear, that the other priest did not?

   Answer: Robe of the Ephod (Blue Robe)

   Ephod

   Breastplate of Judgment

   Urim and Thummim (Exodus 28:5-38)

2) How often did the High Priest enter into the Holy of Holies?

   Answer: Once a year (Leviticus 16:34), (Hebrews 9:7)

3) Which Priestly Garments were worn into the Holy of Holies?

Answer: Holy Linen Coat (Robe of Righteousness)

Linen Breeches

Linen Girdle

Linen Mitre

(Leviticus 16:4)

You may be surprised the Robe of the Ephod, the Ephod, the Breastplate of Judgment with the Urim & Thummim were not worn into the Holy of Holies. We will study this in the next 2 chapters and see why these garments were worn in the Holy Place not the Holy of Holies.

During the time of the Old Covenant, the High Priest went into the Holy of Holies for himself and for everyone else, because the way into the Holiest of all was not yet made manifest while the first Tabernacle was yet standing.

Jesus has made a new and living way for us to be able to come into His presence through His blood that was shed upon Calvary's Cross and presented before God the Father in Heaven itself.

We no longer have to depend upon someone else to come into God's presence for us; although we do have others that unknowingly depend on us to bring them before the Father, because they do not know Him.

CHAPTER 11

The Robe of the Ephod

This will be an in-depth study of the Robe of the Ephod; what it represented and why we have been permitted to wear it spiritually and for what purpose. How blessed we are to be given such a privilege to be endued with power from on high.

1) What color was the Robe of the Ephod?

   Answer: Blue (Exodus 28:31)

2) How was it put on?

   Answer: from above, over the head (Exodus 28:32)

3) Did Aaron put this Garment on by himself?

Answer: No, Moses put it upon him. (Exodus 29:5)

4) Describe the Robe of the Ephod.

Answer: Blue

- • Hole in the top with a woven work round about the hole of it
- • Beneath upon the hem of it are pomegranates of blue, purple, and scarlet round about the hem of it with golden bells between them round about (Exodus 28:31-33)

5) Where was the Robe of the Ephod worn?

Answer: The Holy Place "The Sanctuary" (Exodus 28:35)

6) What was the purpose of the Robe of the Ephod?

Answer: To minister: and his sound shall be heard when he goeth in unto the Holy Place before the Lord, and when he cometh out, that he die not.

7) What sound was heard and what did it represent:

Answer 1: Bells ringing as they hit the pomegranates as the High Priest ministered.

Answer 2: Represents the Gifts of the Spirit through the love of God, in full operation in the Church; "The Holy Place"

8) What New Testament chapter is symbolic of the bells and pomegranates on the bottom of the robe?

Answer: I Corinthians 12 – Bell Chapter, "Gifts of the Spirit

I Corinthians 13 – Pomegranate, "Love Chapter"

I Corinthians 14 – Bell Chapter, "Gifts of the Spirit"

Going forward, let's see how the disciples and others were clothed upon with the Robe of the Ephod and why. Know the foundation truths of God's Word.

9) Did the disciples know anything about the day of Pentecost:

Answer: Yes, it had been celebrated as a Feast Day for years. Fifty days after the Feast of First Fruits.

10) How many days did Jesus show Himself alive after His resurrection?

Answer: 40 days (Acts 1:3)

11) Jesus told the disciples not to depart from the city of Jerusalem, but to wait for the promise of the Father? What was the promise of the Father?

Answer: Ye shall be baptized with the Holy Ghost not many days hence. (Acts 1:5)

12) The disciples returned to Jerusalem and gathered in the upper room for the next 10 days. What was this symbolic of?

Answer: They were to offer a new meat offering unto the Lord; it was to be baked with leaven; it was a Feast Day.

This speaks of a time of preparation for the Day of Pentecost. (Leviticus 23:16-17)

One mind, one accord, prayer and fasting.

And suddenly there came a sound from Heaven as of a rushing mighty wind, and it filled all the house where they were sitting.

And there appeared unto them cloven tongues like as of fire, and it sat upon each of them and they were all filled with the

Holy Ghost, and began to speak with other tongues as the Spirit gave them utterance. (Acts 2:2-4)

This was the promise of the Father, to be baptized in the Holy Ghost; endued with power from on high with the manifestations of the Gifts of the Spirit, being given to all who received Him.

Clothed upon with the Holy Ghost, which was symbolic of the Robe of the Ephod with the bells and pomegranates ringing in the love of God; being manifested in the church.

What happened? What took place here? For only the High Priest was permitted to wear this Garment and it was symbolic of that which was to come.

The way into the Holiest was not yet made manifest, while as the first Tabernacle was yet standing, but we have Jesus, the Author and Finisher of our faith, who gave Himself that we could be redeemed.

Offered His own blood and presented Himself alive before God the Father; not in a Tabernacle made by man but into Heaven itself; the True Tabernacle of God.

Once and for all putting away sin by the sacrifice of Himself and sat down on the right hand of God. For by one offering he hath perfected forever them that are sanctified. (Hebrews 10:14)

Having therefore, brethren boldness, to enter into the Holiest by the blood of Jesus. By a new and living way, which He hath consecrated for us, through the Veil, that is to say, His flesh; and having a **High Priest** over the house of God; let us draw near with a true heart in full assurance of faith, having our hearts sprinkled from an evil conscience, and our bodies washed with the pure water. (Hebrews 10:19-22)

CHAPTER 12

The Ephod

What an honor to be permitted to wear such a garment as the Ephod with the Breastplate of Judgment, those precious stones and the Urim and Thummim inside the pocket of the Breastplate of Judgment.

Let's study the Ephod and know the importance of its purpose; that we may know what we've been equipped with, to fulfill the will of God.

Take this to heart, God has brought us into the Priesthood, because He so loved the world that He gave His only Son, that we could have everlasting life with Him.

He's willing that none should perish and be lost without Him. Live your life and show Christ Jesus to others, bring them before God. He has equipped you, not only with the garments, but also with the love of God that has enabled you to wear them, by the blood of Jesus.

"Share this love with others".

1) What was special about the 2 onyx stones on the shoulders of the Ephod?

Answer: The names of the 12 tribes of Israel was engraved into them. Six tribes on one stone and six tribes on the other stone. (Exodus 28:9-10)

2) What was the purpose of this?

Answer: Aaron shall bear their names before the Lord upon his shoulders for a memorial. (Exodus 28:12)

3) Where was the Breastplate of Judgment placed upon the Ephod?

Answer: Upon the heart (Exodus 29:29)

4) What was the purpose of this?

Answer: Aaron shall bear the judgment of the children of Israel upon his heart before the Lord continually. (Exodus 28:30)

5) Aaron was to bear the names of the children of Israel before the Lord continually; to carry their load, to bear the judgment. What Old Testament scripture having to do with the Priesthood does this remind you of?

Answer: and the Lord said unto Aaron, "thou and thy sons and thy father's house with thee shall bear the iniquity of the Sanctuary: and thou and thy sons with thee shall bear the iniquity of your Priesthood". (Exodus 18:1)

6) What was the Hebrew definition for the Urim and Thummim?

Answer 1: Urim (224/217) lights, an oracular brilliancy of the figures in the High Priest Breastplate - (217) flame, fire

Answer 2: Thummim (8550) Perfections; the object in the High Priest Breastplate as an emblem of complete truth.

7) Where was the Urim and Thummim placed at on the Ephod?

Answer: In the pocket of the Breastplate of Judgment. (Exodus 28:16,30)

8) What was the purpose of the Urim and Thummim?

Answer 1 : To receive council from the Lord. (Numbers 27:21)

Answer 2: That Aaron would bear the judgment of the children of Israel upon his heart before the Lord continually. (Exodus 28:30)

9) Going forward to the New Testament, knowing we have been permitted to wear the Ephod and the Breastplate of Judgment, how is it that we have received the Urim and Thummim to place upon our hearts as we come into the presence of the Lord, not only for ourselves, but also on the behalf of others?

Answer: He shall baptize you with the Holy Ghost, and with Fire. (Matthew 3:11, Luke 3:16, Acts 2:1-4)

The Urim and Thummim was placed in the pocket of the Breastplate of Judgment behind the 12 precious stones, which were set in gold enclosures and the names of the 12 tribes of Israel were engraved into them. This must have truly been a sight to see, the light from the Urim, shining against the backside of the precious stones, set in the gold settings and causing them to glow and sparkle as the light shined through them.

God is so good, just imagine the sparkle and glow from those stones to catch someone's eye as the High Priest would continue to minister on the outside of the Tabernacle.

These Garments were for the people. They were to be worn as Aaron went into the Holy Place, the Sanctuary, and when he came out, that he would not die. (Exodus 28:35)

The Hebrew definition of the Ephod (646) is the High Priest Shoulder Piece, also an Image.

You and I have been equipped with and permitted to wear these garments; after all we have been made in the image of God and His Son, Jesus, and after their likeness, even as it's written in Genesis 1:26.

As we wear these garments and come into the very presence of God not just for ourselves but on the behalf of others; bearing them and their circumstances upon our shoulders and over our hearts, we then bear the image of God as we intercede on their behalf.

The glory of God is upon us that we would be one with them, that the world may believe that God sent His Son, Jesus. (John 12:21)

CHAPTER 13

The Laver

1) **Where was the Laver located?**

   Answer: Thou shalt put it between the Tabernacle of Congregation and the Altar. (Exodus 30:18)

2) **What was the Laver made from?**

   Answer: The brass looking glasses of the women. (Exodus 38:8)

3) **How often did Aaron and his sons have to wash their hands and feet at the Laver?**

   Answer: When they went into the Tabernacle and when they came near to the Altar to minister. (Exodus 30:20)

4) What was washing their hands and feet symbolic of?

Answer: That He might sanctify and cleanse it with the washing of water by the Word. That He might present it to Himself a glorious church, not having spot or wrinkle, or any such thing; but that it should be holy and without blemish. (Ephesians 5: 26 & 27)

CHAPTER 14

The Door of the Tabernacle

1) What did the Door of the Tabernacle represent?

   Answer: Truth (John 14:6)

2) Why were the 5 sockets that 5 pillars sit on made of brass or copper?

   Answer: because they were still on the Courtyard side of the Door. (Exodus 26:37)

3) What did the 5 pillars covered in gold represent?

   Answer: I believe they represent man trying to fulfill the law of God, yet being unable to and therefore, the sockets were of brass, which represent judgment.

CHAPTER 15

The Tabernacle Structure

I have many favorite parts of the Tabernacle and the Tabernacle Structure is one of them because of the amount of detail God has given us, to show us how much He loves us and how He holds us secure in His love.

1) What type of wood was used to build the Tabernacle and what did it represent?

   Answer: Shittim wood (Exodus 26:15) representing humanity (Mark 8:24 & Isaiah 61:3)

2) What's the Hebrew definition for Shittim wood and what was the size of each board?

   Answer 1: (7838) scourging thorns

(7850) to pierce

(7752) to flog, goad, scourge

Answer 2: 10 cubits tall = 15 feet, cubit and ½ wide = 27" (Exodus 26:16)

3) What was the foundation that each board sat on, what did it weigh, and what did it represent?

Answer 1: Two sockets of silver under each board (Exodus 26:19, 21, 25)

Answer 2: One socket weighed 1 talent = 75 pounds (Exodus 38:27)

Answer 3: Silver represents redemption or redeemed.

4) What held the boards secure, in place, on the Sockets of Silver and what did they represent?

Answer 1: One tenon per socket of silver.

Answer 2: Tenon (3027) a hand, power, strength, assistance

5) **What did this represent?**

   Answer: The two hands of God, holding us secure in the redemptive work of Christ Jesus that took place at Calvary.

6) **How did the boards sit in order and what did this represent?**

   Answer 1: one against another (Exodus 26:17)

   Answer 2: represents unity, a oneness, relationship

7) **The Tabernacle was 15 feet wide and Exodus 26:25 says there were 8 boards and 16 sockets of silver on the west end; the backside. The boards were 18 inches wide. How did they make this work?**

   Answer: They used 6 full sized 27 "boards and two 9" boards; one for each corner. (Exodus 26:22-23)

8) **What did the two 9" boards represent?**

   Answer: The boards represented humanity; the two smaller boards represent someone that doesn't feel like they measure up, or someone going through hard times, or someone with a sickness of some type. These are the hurting within the church. God places them in the corner because it's the strongest part of the Structure.

9) There were 16 Sockets of Silver, two sockets under every board and according to Exodus 38:27 each Socket of Silver was made of one talent of silver, which is 75 pounds. How did they make this work for the two 9" boards in the corners?

Answer: Do we speculate to get this answer or maybe just use logic and say they cut the Sockets of Silver down to fit their boards. No, can't imagine that, especially since these Sockets of Silver represent the Redemptive work of Christ Jesus. I believe we stay with Scripture that we know and that's Exodus 38:27, that each socket was made of one talent of silver. The Sockets of Silver under the two 9" boards had a tenon in each of them just like all the other boards and must have extended out beyond the other sockets, creating a more secure foundation.

Just like God to place the hurting in the strongest part of the building and to create an even more secure foundation. God doesn't stop there. He continues to show His love by joining them to the others.

10) The two corner boards were to be Coupled Together (8382) beneath and coupled together above the head of it unto one ring. What was the purpose of this and what did it represent?

Answer: The ring joined the small board to the large full-sized board next to it, that it would have its support and be as strong as the others.

Coupled Together (8382) To be complete, to be doubled, paired, to be twins, duplicate.

Again, we see, we are not just talking about boards, this is representing the Church; the body of Christ Jesus reaching out to the hurting or someone with hardships and supporting them with God's love.

Galatians 6:1,2, Brethren, if a man be overtaken in a fault, ye which are spiritual, restore such a one in the spirit of meekness; considering thyself, lest thou also be tempted. Bear ye one another's burdens, and so fulfill the law of God.

11) The Tabernacle was 15 feet tall, sitting on solid blocks of silver. What kept the boards all in line and straight with one another towards the top and what did this represent?

Answer: Five bars of Shittim wood slide through the gold rings mounted to the boards which kept them aligned.

Represents the Five-Fold Ministry of God's Apostles, Prophets, Evangelists, Pastors and Teachers for the perfecting of the Saints, for the work of the ministry, for the edifying of the body of Christ.

CHAPTER 16

The Lampstand

1) What was the Lampstand and the vessels they used for it made of?

   Answer: One talent of pure gold. (Exodus 25:31,39)

2) What was the Lampstand used for ; what purpose?

   Answer: To provide light for the priest in the Holy Place.

3) What scripture references relates the Lampstand to the Word of God?

   Answer: Thy word is a lamp unto my feet and a light unto my path. (Psalm 119:105)

4) Some of the ornaments were shaped like unto almonds. What does this represent?

Answer: The quick work of God. (Jeremiah 1:11-12)

5) How many ornaments were in the Lampstand and what do they represent?

Answer: 66 ornaments, represent the 66 books of the Bible

6) What was special about the shaft of the Lampstand, what was its purpose and what did it represent?

Answer 1: A place for the priest's hand, to carry it.

Answer 2: Making an oath with God, that we are committed to keeping His Word.

CHAPTER 17

The Table of Shewbread

1) What was the Table of Shewbread made from and overlaid with what? What did this represent?

Answer 1: Shittim wood which represented humanity

Answer 2: Overlaid with gold and represented the Glory of God.

Overlay (6823) expansion in outlook; peer into the distance. God who quickeneth the dead, and calleth those things which be not as though they were. (Romans 4:17)

2) What is the border of the Table of Shewbread? What is it for and what does it represent?

Answer 1: Border (4526) enclosing, a close place, a stronghold

Answer 2: It is where the Shewbread was placed.

Answer 3: Represents a close place of intimacy with God.

And it came to pass, as He sat at meat with them, He took the bread, and blessed it, and broke, and gave to them. And their eyes were opened, and they knew Him: and He vanished out of their sight. (Luke 24:30,31)

3) The Table of Shewbread was made of wood overlaid in gold, but the dishes thereof were made of pure gold. Why was this and what did it represent?

Answer 1: Everything used upon the Table to minister unto the Lord had to be of pure gold that the Shewbread would always be upon the Table.

Answer 2: Representing everything within our lives needs to be pure and holy, that Jesus remains within us.

CHAPTER 18

The Golden Altar

1) What was the Golden Altar made from and overlaid with? What did this represent?

Answer 1: Shittim wood which represented humanity.

Answer 2: Overlaid with gold, represented the Glory of God.

Overlay (6823) expansion in outlook, peer into the distance.
God who quickeneth the dead, and calleth those things which be not as though they were. (Romans 4:17)

2) What was the purpose of the Golden Altar and what did it represent?

Answer 1: To burn incense upon every morning and evening as they tend to the Lampstand. (Exodus 30:7,8)

Answer 2: Represents the prayers of the saints ascending up before God.

Psalm 141: Let my prayer be set forth before thee as incense. (see Revelation 8:3,4)

3) Where did the Golden Altar sit at within the Tabernacle?

Answer: Put it before the Veil that is by the Ark of the Testimony (Exodus 30:6)

4) How was the Golden Altar carried throughout the wilderness? How was it supported and what did it represent?

Answer 1: It was supported by two rings on opposite corners of the Golden Altar, which allowed the Altar to stay level as they carried it.

Answer 2: With the two rings being what supports the Golden Altar as they travel the wilderness. The purpose of the Altar is to burn incense, which represents prayer and intercession, the two rings would represent Jesus and the Holy Ghost which intercedes before God, for us. (Romans 8:26-27,34)

CHAPTER 19

The Incense

1) **What is the name of the sweet spices that were used to make the Incense?**

   Answer: Stacte, Onycha, Galbanum, Frankincense

2) **How was the mixture of the spices to be used?**

   Answer: of each shall be a like weight (Exodus 30:34)

3) **What was the name of the profession of mixing these together?**

   Answer: The Art of the Apothecary; a perfumer. (Exodus 30:35)

4) God gave the mixture of Incense a name. What was it and what did it represent?

Answer 1: Perfume (7004) a fumigation; a sweet-smelling odor when it is burned.

Answer 2: Represented our prayers ascending up before God, driving out all the distractions, as this place of prayer is filled with praise and the needs of ourselves and others are presented before God.

There's much to be gleaned from the process of gathering and harvesting this four-part composition of Incense. I suggest your own Word study to be done, as I myself, also will continue to do; in order to appreciate and to know what it takes to bring ourselves and others before God. There was time and effort put into this process and it is symbolic of our brokenness and hardships as well as compassion and understanding for others.

CHAPTER 20

The Holy Place

1) **What was another name for the Holy Place?**

   Answer: The Sanctuary (Exodus 25:8)

2) **What furniture was placed within the Holy Place and what was this symbolic of?**

   Answer 1: Lampstand – Word of God

   Golden Altar – Prayer

   Table of Shewbread — Communion

   Answer 2: Symbolic of the Word of God, communion, prayers and intercession being in full operation in the church.

And they continued steadfastly in the Apostle's doctrine and fellowship and in breaking of bread, and in prayer. (Acts 2:42)

3) As a reminder, what is the foundation within the Holy Place?

Answer: Solid blocks of silver, representing the redemptive work of Christ, with the two hands of God; Jesus and the Holy Ghost holding us secure in His love.

CHAPTER 21

The Tabernacle Coverings

1) **What was the size of the Tabernacle?**

   Answer 1: 15 feet wide, 15 feet tall, and 45 feet long

2) **What was the size of the first inner covering?**

   Answer: 28 cubits = 42 feet

   4 cubits deep = 6 feet

   (Exodus 26:2)

3) **How many curtains made up the inner covering?**

   Answer: 10 (Exodus 26:1)

4) How many curtains covered the Holy Place and how many covered the Holy of Holies?

Answer 1: 5 covered the Holy Place

Answer 2: 5 covered the Holy of Holies (Exodus 26:3)

5) How were the curtains connected together and what did this represent?

Answer: One (802) to another (269)

One (802) woman, wife, a bride
Another (269) sister, brother, your spouse, one of an intimate relationship (Exodus 26:3)

Take the time to notice and discuss what God has given us here in the Scriptures. He's showing us the unity and fellowship of the Church; the body of Christ.

To pray ye one for another, to support each other and be joined together as one.

6) Where did the 5 curtains over the Holy Place connect to the 5 curtains over the Holy of Holies?

Answer: Over the Veil, which separated the Holy of Holies from the Holy Place.

7) How were the 5 curtains over the Holy Place connected to the 5 curtains over the Holy of Holies and what did this represent?

Answer: 50 loops of blue are upon the edge of both curtains and the 50 loops from each side take hold of one another. There were also 50 taches of gold which took hold of the loops of blue, creating one Tabernacle.

How beautiful is this. I pray that everyone will pause and see the glory of God, the love of God, that He has for us and His intent, is for us to be one with Him.

The way into the Holiest was not yet made manifest while as the first Tabernacle was yet standing. (Hebrews 9:8) and yet all these years before Jesus came here to live amongst us and fulfill His Father's will; God is showing us, of that which was to come; using the Tabernacle and the Priesthood.

The Veil was there to separate the Holy of Holies from the Holy Place, because mankind had not yet been made worthy to come into the very presence of God. That was yet to come, once we would be washed in the blood of Jesus.

The 50 loops of blue taking hold one of another, connecting the Holy Place to the Holy of Holies; creating one Tabernacle, represents the Holy Ghost joining us, of the church age, within the Holy Place to the Holy of Holies, which represents the kingdom of Heaven.

Also notice the joining of these took place right over top of the Veil, which represents Jesus' body.

Beautiful, beautiful Scripture!

My heart yearns to describe this better, but just know that God desires you and I to be one with Him and Jesus, that others can see Christ Jesus in us; that they too would believe that God has sent Him. (see the Scriptures, John 17:21-23)

CHAPTER 22

The Veil

1) **What was the purpose of the Veil?**

   Answer: To separate the Holy Place from the Holy of Holies, that God could dwell among His people.

2) **What was the Veil attached to? What was its foundation and what did this represent?**

   Answer: The Veil was attached to the 4 pillars overlaid with gold, which sat upon 4 sockets of silver. The 4 pillars represented humanity, Matthew, Mark, Luke and John, which received and wrote the 4 Gospels in which the New Covenant is established upon, and therefore man is being

enabled to be obedient unto the Gospel through the grace of God and the blood of our Lord Jesus Christ.

3) There were 50 loops of blue that joined the Holy Place to the Holy of Holies, just above the Veil. What did this represent?

Answer: This represented the promise of God to come, that the Holy Place and the Holy of Holies would become one Tabernacle; referring to the Church becoming one with God and our Lord Jesus Christ.

This happens by the blood of Jesus Christ, (the Veil), and the Holy Ghost, (50 loops of blue), which we were sealed with, the Holy Spirit of Promise, which is the earnest of our inheritance until the redemption of the purchased possession, unto the praise of His glory. The 50 loops of blue taking hold of one of another and the taches of gold holding them together, representing us, the Church, being made one with God and our Lord Jesus Christ. (See John 17:21-23)

Studying the blue color of the Veil seems to have to do with the suffering that Jesus bore upon the Cross.

Study the process to get the blue dye and study the Scriptures in Psalm 22. There's more to see here, which will require more time of study and prayer.

4) What does the red color of the Veil represent?

Answer: The blood of Jesus.

5) How did they get the scarlet (8144, 8438), red color?

Answer: Extracted from the crimson grub worm.

Take the time to study the scarlet, Hebrew definition of the word, along with the Scriptures in Psalm 22:6

The blue and scarlet red colors in the Veil are beautiful, beautiful descriptions of God's love for us, through the sacrifice that His Son, Jesus has done and given to us; and that's His life, that we might have life and have it more abundantly. Please take the time and recognize His goodness and His great love for us. The story of the crimson grub worm is symbolic of us partaking of Jesus' body through communion. The maggot worm is symbolic of Jesus, knowing exactly where and what the sin is that may still be hidden within us. God loves us that much that He won't let it remain. Saints, it's coming out, give it to Him, He knows you and He loves you!

CHAPTER 23

The Placement of the Veil

1) The veil represented Jesus' body and separated the Holy Place from the Holy of Holies. Why was this needed in order for God to dwell among His people?

   Answer: Because the way into the Holiest of all was not yet made manifest, while as the first Tabernacle was yet standing. (Hebrews 9:8)

2) When Jesus died upon the Cross, what took place in the Temple and what did this represent?

   Answer: The Veil of the Temple was rent in twain from top to bottom ... (Matthew 27:51)

Representing the way into the Holiest of all has now been made manifest to man.

Having therefore, brethren, boldness to enter into the Holiest by the blood of Jesus, by a new and living way, which He hath consecrated for us, through the Veil, that is to say His flesh. (Hebrews 10:19-20)

3) We have been given access into the very presence of God by the blood of Jesus; all sin has been forgiven, the power of sin has been broken, and we have been redeemed and the Spirit of God lives within us. What other blessing / benefit have we received because of the blood of Jesus; to cause us to be able to serve the Living God?

Answer: He has purged our conscience from dead works to serve the Living God. (Hebrews 9:14)

CHAPTER 24

The Ark of the Covenant

1) What was the Ark of the Covenant made of and what did it represent?

   Answer: Shittim wood, representing humanity

2) It was overlaid with pure gold within and without. What did this represent?

   Answer: The glory of God on the inside of us and the outside.

   Overlay (6823) expansion in outlook, to peer into the distance

3) What New Testament scripture would this reflect upon?

Answer: ... God who quickeneth the dead, and calleth those things which be not as though they were. (Romans 4: 17)

4) What was kept inside the Ark of the Covenant and what did they each represent?

Answer: Ten Commandments – Father (Exodus 25:16)

Golden Pot of Manna – Jesus (John 6:48-51)

Rod of Aaron that budded – Holy Ghost (Numbers 17:10 and

Hebrews 9:4)

5) Understanding question #4, what is this promise of God we've been given in the Old Testament Tabernacle?

Answer: That man would be changed inside and out and dwell in the very presence of God; and the Father, Son and Holy Ghost would dwell inside of man. "Hallelujah, God be praised!"

6) What's the name of the lid of the Ark of the Covenant and what does it represent?

Answer: Mercy Seat and it represents Jesus as our propitiation (Exodus 25:17-20) and (Romans 3:25-26)

The Mercy Seat was the lid of the Ark of the Covenant and was a perfect fit over the Ark, being the same size; which caused it to seal in the items God had placed inside.

Jesus is now the Mercy Seat and has sealed us with the Holy Spirit of Promise!

CHAPTER 25

The Journey through
the Wilderness

1) How did the children of Israel know when it was time to disassemble the Tabernacle and move?

Answer: When the cloud was taken up from over the Tabernacle. (Exodus 40:36-38)

2) What was done first in the disassembling the Tabernacle and who did it?

Answer: Aaron and his sons were to take down the Veil and cover the Ark of the Covenant with the Veil.

As you read in the book, Into His Presence, the Veil was probably folded to cover the Ark so it didn't touch the ground as they traveled through the wilderness. Just to clarify, we don't have an exact size of the height of the Mercy Seat and the Angels; also, I believe the Veil was a bit smaller than the 15 feet by 15 feet, because the Tabernacle dimension of the 15-foot width would have been to the outside of the structure, which would allow for the coverings overhead to fit properly according to the Scriptures. We also are not given the exact size of the Veil; although it did seal off the area of the Holy Place from the Holy of Holies. The width would have been just shy of the thickness of the boards of the Tabernacle and the height would have probably been the same, which would allow the smoke from the Incense to go up over the Veil and into the presence of God.

This being said the Veil would still have been a perfect fit; a covering for the Ark of the Covenant.

3) There were 6 wagons and 12 oxen given unto the Levites for the service of the Tabernacle, but none was given unto the sons of Kohath, because the service of the Sanctuary belonging unto them was that they should bear upon their shoulders. They were to carry the Ark of the Covenant, Table of Shewbread, Laver and the Brazen Altar. What was the purpose of this and what did it represent?

Answer:

The Ark of the Covenant with the covering Veil would represent us staying in covenant relationship with God as we move through this wilderness.

The Golden Altar, the prayers of the saints, the Lampstand, the Word of God in our lives.

The Table of Shewbread, us keeping communion with God.

The Brazen Altar us recognizing what Jesus has done for us and picking up our cross daily and following Him.

The Laver reminding us that we need to be washed and cleansed daily, by the washing of water by the Word.

God bless you, my brothers and sisters in Christ!

Printed in the United States
by Baker & Taylor Publisher Services